A Dollar Bill's Journey

by Suzanne Slade

illustrated by Susan Swan

PICTURE WINDOW BOOKS

a capstone imprint

Thanks to our advisers for their expertise, research, and advice:

Klaus Becker, PhD, Associate Professor and Interim Chair
Department of Economics and Geography
Texas Tech University

Terry Flaherty, PhD, Professor of English
Minnesota State University, Mankato

Editor: Jill Kalz
Designer: Tracy Davies
Art Director: Nathan Gassman
Production Specialist: Sarah Bennett
The illustrations in this book were created with mixed media/found object.

Picture Window Books
151 Good Counsel Drive
P.O. Box 669
Mankato, MN 56002-0669
877-845-8392
www.capstonepub.com

All books published by Picture Window Books are manufactured
with paper containing at least 10 percent post-consumer waste.

Library of Congress Cataloging-in-Publication Data
Slade, Suzanne.
 A dollar bill's journey / by Suzanne Slade ; illustrated by Susan Swan.
   p. cm.
 Includes index.
 ISBN 978-1-4048-6265-4 (library binding) — ISBN 978-1-4048-6709-3 (paperback)
 1. Dollar, American—United States. 2. Paper money—United
States—Juvenile literature. I. Swan, Susan, 1944– II. Title.
 HG591.S62 2011
 332.4'973—dc22   2010033768

Printed in the United States of America in North Mankato, Minnesota.
092010
005933CGS11

Whir! Clack! Clink!

Something exciting is happening at the Bureau of Printing and Engraving in Washington, D.C.

A giant stack of paper stands ready. Metal plates are coated with ink. Huge cutting blades wink in the light.

A dollar bill is about to be born.

Making money is a long, difficult process. All U.S. paper money goes through more than 65 steps before it's ready to be used.

I'm one in 800 billion!

The dollar bill's journey begins with a piece of soft steel. Artists carve words and pictures into it.

The carved metal is used to make printing plates. Coated with ink, these heavy plates press hard into each sheet of paper. The dollar bill gets its green back first.

Green is SO in this year!

The ink on U.S. paper money is used only by the U.S. Department of the Treasury. The special ink helps to keep people from making fake bills.

After drying for a day or two, the sheets are printed with their black front. A huge blade slices the stack in two.

Workers look carefully at each sheet. If the bills look OK, they're numbered and stamped with a seal.

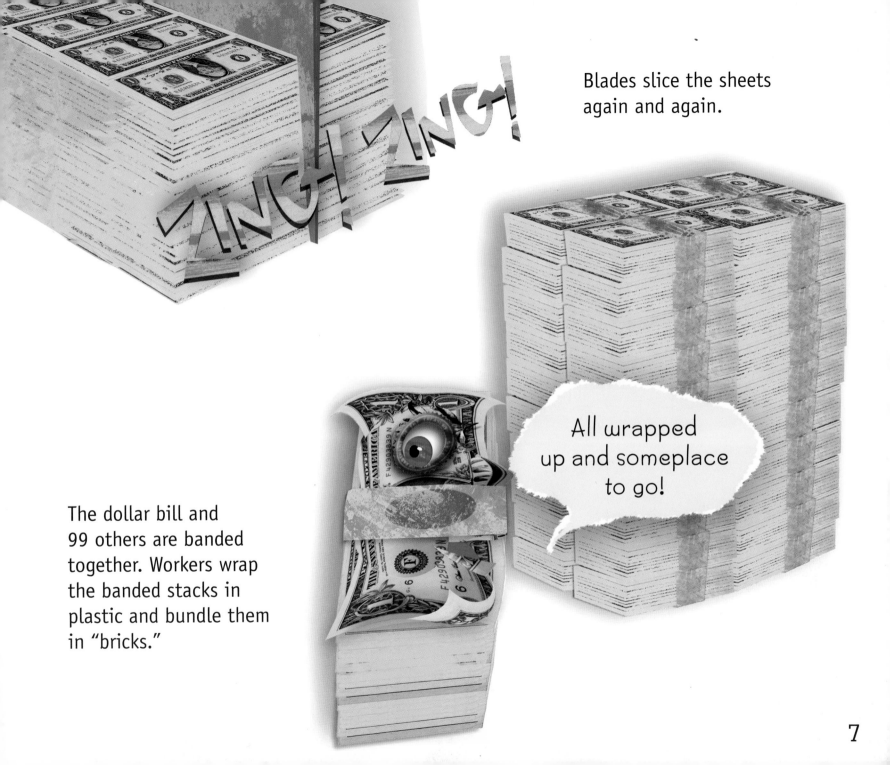

Blades slice the sheets again and again.

ZING! ZING!

The dollar bill and 99 others are banded together. Workers wrap the banded stacks in plastic and bundle them in "bricks."

All wrapped up and someplace to go!

7

The dollar bill bounces down the road in an armored truck. First stop? The Federal Reserve Bank in Chicago.

Guards carry the bags of bills inside. There the dollar bill waits ... and waits.

Who turned out the lights?

But before long, it's loaded into another truck.
Next stop? A commercial bank a few hours away.

New U.S. bills must go through one of the 12 Federal
Reserve Banks. These banks supply money to about
9,400 commercial banks across the country.

Now the fun *really* begins. A woman rushes into the commercial bank and takes out some money. She stuffs the dollar bill and a few others inside a card. She can't be late for the party!

Suddenly, the dollar bill is face-to-face with a happy girl.

After lunch, the birthday girl gives the dollar bill to a man in a ticket booth.

He later hands the bill to a boy as change. The boy stuffs it into his pocket and heads for the Racing Rocket.

The next morning, the boy throws his dirty clothes in the wash. The dollar bill gets an unexpected bath.

swish! swish! swish!

The dollar bill starts spinning around ... and around ... and around.

Buzzzz!

The boy plucks out the dollar bill and hangs it in the sun to dry.

Jiffy mart

Soon the boy gets thirsty. He grabs the dollar bill and runs to the gas station. There he trades the bill for a cold drink.

U.S. paper money is printed on paper made of 75 percent cotton and 25 percent linen. The two fibers together make strong bills that don't fall apart when wet.

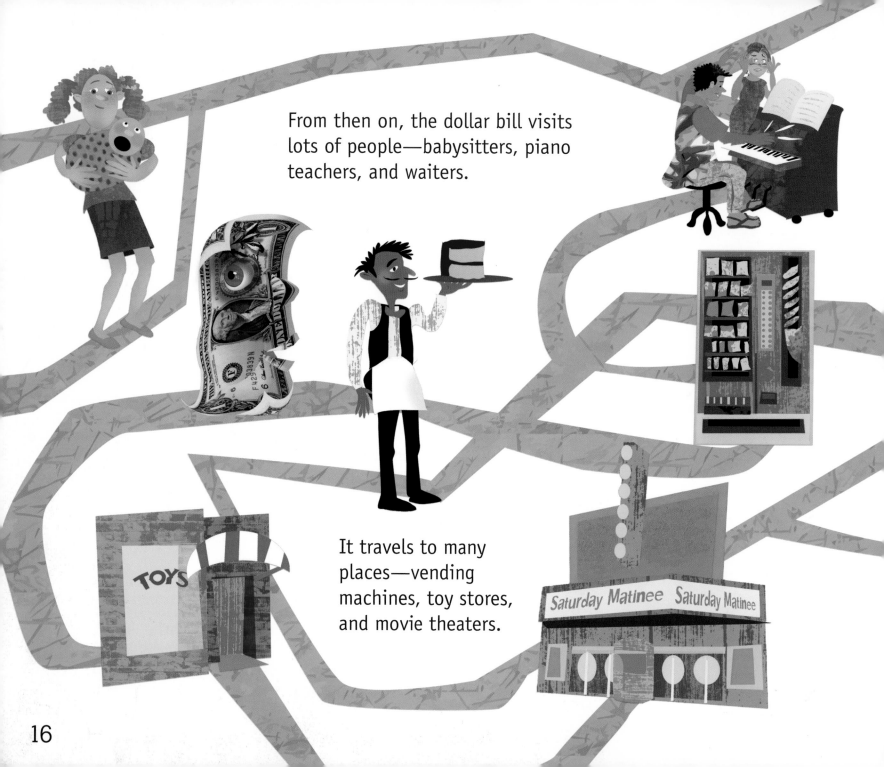

From then on, the dollar bill visits lots of people—babysitters, piano teachers, and waiters.

It travels to many places—vending machines, toy stores, and movie theaters.

TOYS

Saturday Matinee Saturday Matinee

And it pays for all kinds of things—ice cream, apples, and overdue books.

Whew! I love to travel, but this is crazy!

The U.S. Department of the Treasury produces more than 2.5 billion dollar bills a year. Bills are printed in Washington, D.C., and Fort Worth, Texas. Each dollar bill costs about 6.5 cents to make.

After many months, the dollar bill is wrinkled and worn. Its edges are ripped. Finally, someone returns the bill to a bank.

Packed with other old bills, the dollar bill travels back to a Federal Reserve Bank. It's shredded and tightly pressed with other bill strips to form a paper brick.

But the journey isn't over yet!

Hey, quit crowding me, dude.

Most dollar bills last about 21 months before they are replaced with new bills. The five-dollar bill has an even shorter life span—about 16 months. But 100-dollar bills last about 80 months!

A truck carries the bricks to a factory. The old paper money is recycled into beautiful stationery.

Sometime later, a woman buys the stationery in a card shop. She can't be late for the party!

I was ready for a change.

Old dollar bills are recycled into many things. They may become stationery, insulation for houses, or roof shingles. Some people make art from shredded bills.

Diagram of a Dollar Bill's Journey

Glossary

armored truck—a truck with thick walls and special locks made to keep what it carries safe

carve—to shape something by cutting it

commercial—having to do with a business

Federal Reserve Bank—one of the 12 large banks that make up the Federal Reserve System in the United States

recycle—to turn used goods, such as newspapers or soda cans, into new products

seal—an official mark

U.S. Department of the Treasury—a federal department that manages government money; the Bureau of Engraving and Printing within the Department of the Treasury prints new bills, while the U.S. Mint makes coins

To Learn More

More Books to Read

Clifford, Tim. *How Coins and Bills Are Made.* The Study of Money. Vero Beach, Fla.: Rourke Pub., 2009.

Forest, Christopher. *The Dollar Bill in Translation: What It Really Means.* Kids' Translations. Mankato, Minn.: Capstone Press, 2009.

Internet Sites

FactHound offers a safe, fun way to find Internet sites related to this book. All of the sites on FactHound have been researched by our staff.

Here's all you do:
Visit *www.facthound.com*
Type in this code: 9781404862654

Check out projects, games and lots more at
www.capstonekids.com

Index

Look for all the books in the Follow It series:

A Dollar Bill's Journey

A Germ's Journey

A Plastic Bottle's Journey

A Raindrop's Journey